POEMS for WEE ONES

by MaryAnn Diorio
Illustrations by Valeria Wicker

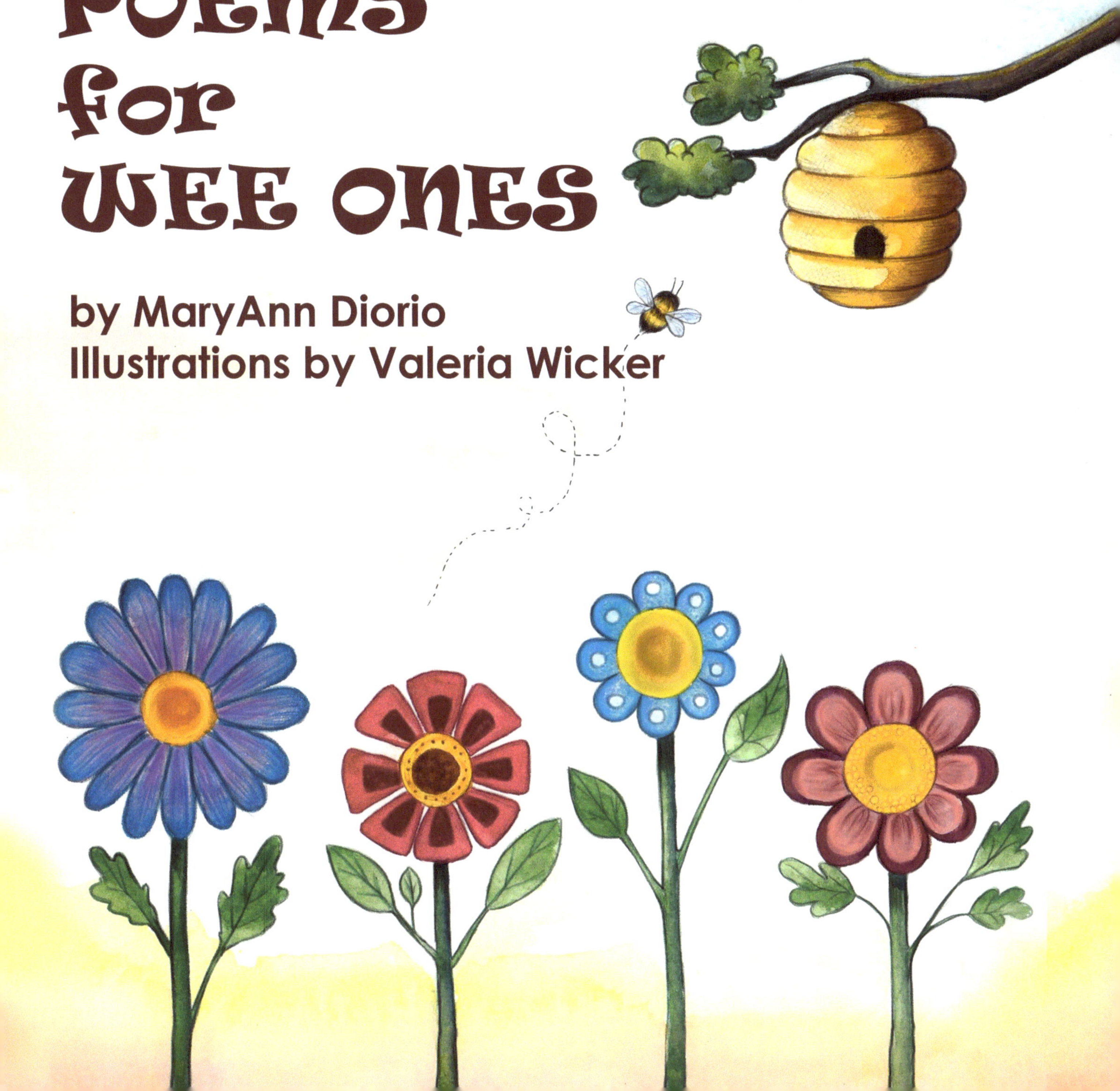

POEMS FOR WEE ONES
Published by TopNotch Press
A Division of MaryAnn Diorio Books
PO Box 1185 Merchantville, NJ 08109

Copyright 2018 by MaryAnn Diorio, PhD. All Rights Reserved.

This publication—or any part thereof—may not be reproduced, scanned, stored in, or introduced into a retrieval system, or transmitted or distributed, in any printed or electronic form, or by any means (electronic, mechanical, photocopying, recording, or otherwise) without the prior written permission of the copyright owner, author, and publisher of this book, Dr. MaryAnn Diorio. Please do not participate in or encourage piracy of copyrighted materials in violation of the author's rights. Purchase only authorized editions.

Hardcover Edition: ISBN: 978-0-930037-50-5
Softcover Edition: ISBN: 978-0-930037-51-2
Electronic Edition: ISBN: 978-0-930037-52-9
Library of Congress Control Number: 2018903354

Illustrated by Valeria Wicker
Edited by Annamarie Joy Gerken

"To my precious grandchildren...

...And to Jesus Who gave them to me."

–MaryAnn Diorio

POEMS ARE . . .

Poems are like jelly beans,
Colorful and chewy,
Some are sweet and some are not,
And some are rather gooey.

WINTER'S WALK

Winter walked a snowy walk
Straight to my hometown,
Bringing with her flakes of white
For spreading all around.

Some she sprinkled on my house,
Some atop the trees,
Some she scattered in my yard,
High up to my knees!

ON SIMPSON STREET

On Simpson Street
There lived a cat
Who played the drums—
Rat-tat-tat-tat.

Next door to her
There lived a bee
Who played the fiddle—
Fiddle-dee-dee.

Across the street
There lived a mole
Who played the flute
With all his soul.

Around the bend
There lived a dog
Who played the trumpet
On a log.

And down the block,
Where hamsters dwell,
A hamster danced
A jig quite well.

Atop the tree
There lived a jay
Who played the violin
All day.

Beneath a roof,
There lived an owl
Who said, "Let's start
An orchestra now!"

So, then, the hamster,
Dog, and mole
Began to play
Around a pole.

Their music drew
The cat and bee,
And now they all
Play happily.

ADD-A-DOG

I have one dog,
Lying-in-the-sun dog,
I have one dog,
My sister has two.

Two dogs, new dogs,
Paddle-a-canoe dogs,
Playing peek-a-boo dogs,
My cousin has three.

Three dogs, free dogs,
Run-around-a-tree dogs,
Chasing bumble-bee dogs,
My Granny has four.

Four dogs, tour dogs,
Slide-across-the-floor dogs,
Swinging on-the-door dogs,
My teacher has five.

Five dogs, live dogs,
Jam-and-jump-and-jive dogs,
Dip-and-drip-and-dive dogs,
Now what do you think of that?

RAINY DAYS

Rainy days are fun days,
Hiding-from-the-sun days,
Wiggle days, jiggle days,
Got-to-give-a-giggle days.

Rainy days are laugh days,
Run-like-a-giraffe days,
Cuddle days, huddle days,
Hop-atop-a-puddle days.

THE TROLLEY

How wonderfully jolly to ride on the trolley,
To sit by the window and watch people pass.
It's really amusing to see them perusing
Me smiling back at them through my window glass.

The rollicking motion does give me a notion
Of being at sea on a ship great and wide,
While passengers sway back and forth all the way,
Standing up in the aisle side by side.

TODAY I SAW A SUNBEAM

Today I saw a sunbeam
And chased it all through town.
I followed it right up a tree,
Then followed it back down.

Today I saw a rainbow
Stretched out across the sky.
I followed it from end to end,
Then waved a grand good-bye.

ANIMACTIVITIES

Kangaroos jump,
Camels bump.
Rabbits hop,
Elephants clop.

Seagulls glide,
Seals slide.
Deer bound,
Whales sound.

Bears lumber,
Koalas slumber.
Swallows dive,
Bees hive.

Lambs frisk,
Gerbils whisk.
Giraffes bleat,
Robins tweet.

Wolves lope,
Lions scope.
Puppies paddle,
Redstarts rattle.

THE ELEPHANT AND THE TREE

Once there was an elephant
Who sat atop a tree.
He ate a bag of peanuts
That he found behind his knee.

He licked a cherry lollipop
That flew in with a bee,
And then he swung his trunk around
And laughed aloud with glee!

SILLY, DILLY PUMPKIN

Silly, Dilly Pumpkin,
Hiding in the patch,
Playing "Come and Find Me,"
See if you can catch
All the little pumpkins
Hiding here with me.
Silly, Dilly Pumpkin,
Silly, Dilly Me!

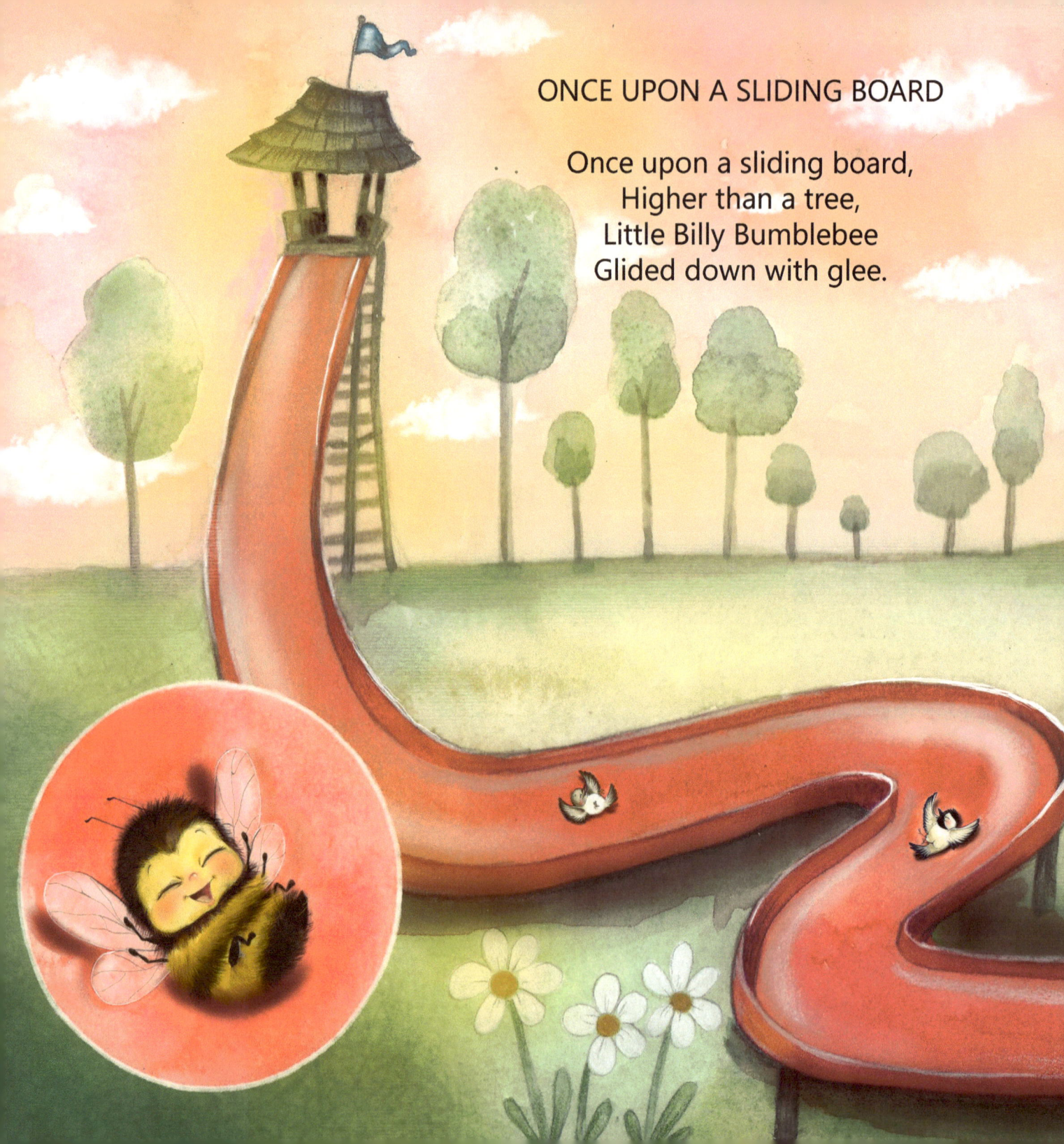

ONCE UPON A SLIDING BOARD

Once upon a sliding board,
Higher than a tree,
Little Billy Bumblebee
Glided down with glee.

Once upon a sliding board,
Higher than a tree,
Little Jennie Nightingale
Twittered, "Look at me!"

Once upon a sliding board,
Higher than a tree,
Little Charlie Chickadee
Slid and shouted, "Whee!"

HANDS

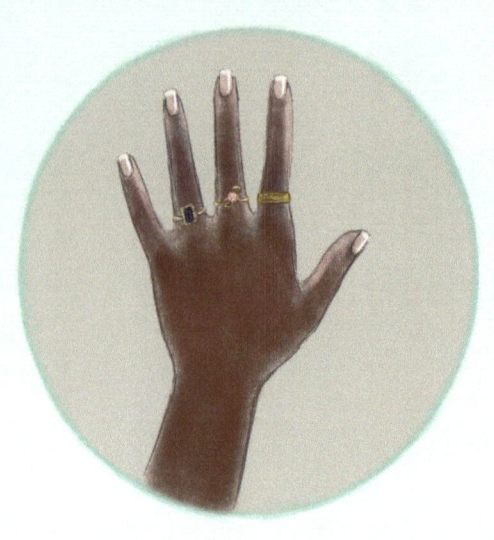

Hands can do
so many things.
They comb the hair
and wear fine rings
and wash the face
and blow the nose
and brush the teeth
and touch the toes.

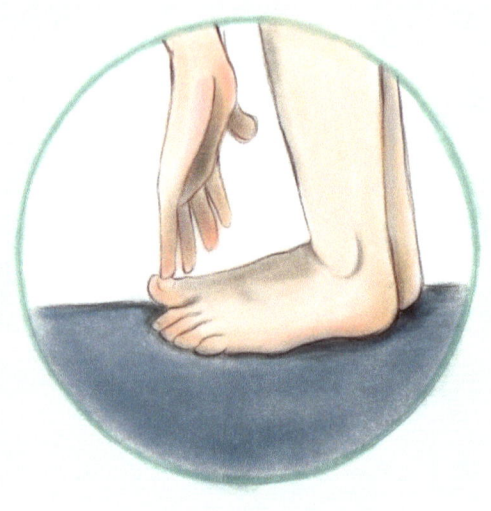

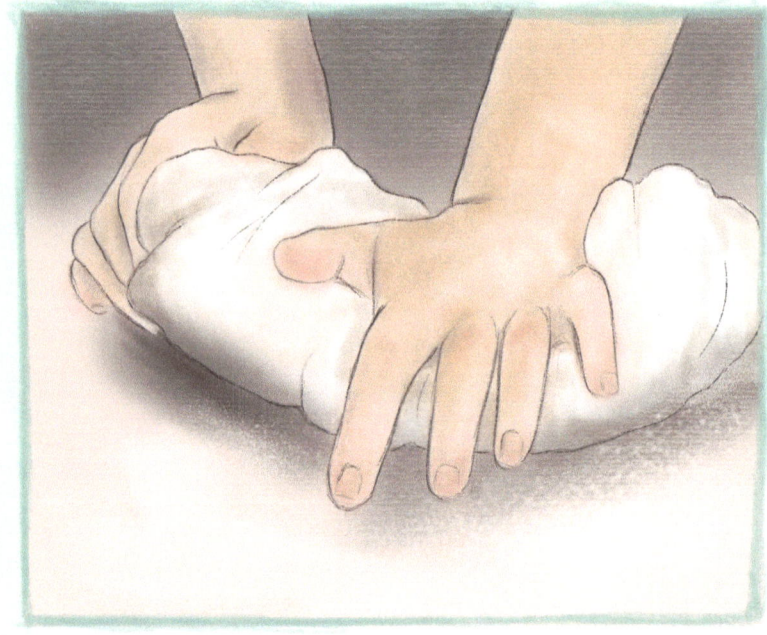

They play the harp
and paint the barn
and cook the meal
and knit the yarn
and knead the dough
and scrub the floor
and fold the clothes
and help the poor.

They tie a knot
And milk the cow
And string the beads
And pull the plough
And dig a hole
And sew the patch
And cut the bread
And pull the latch.

They pet the dog
and make the bed
and push the swing
and scratch the head
and write the note
and plant the seed
and give a gift
to those in need.

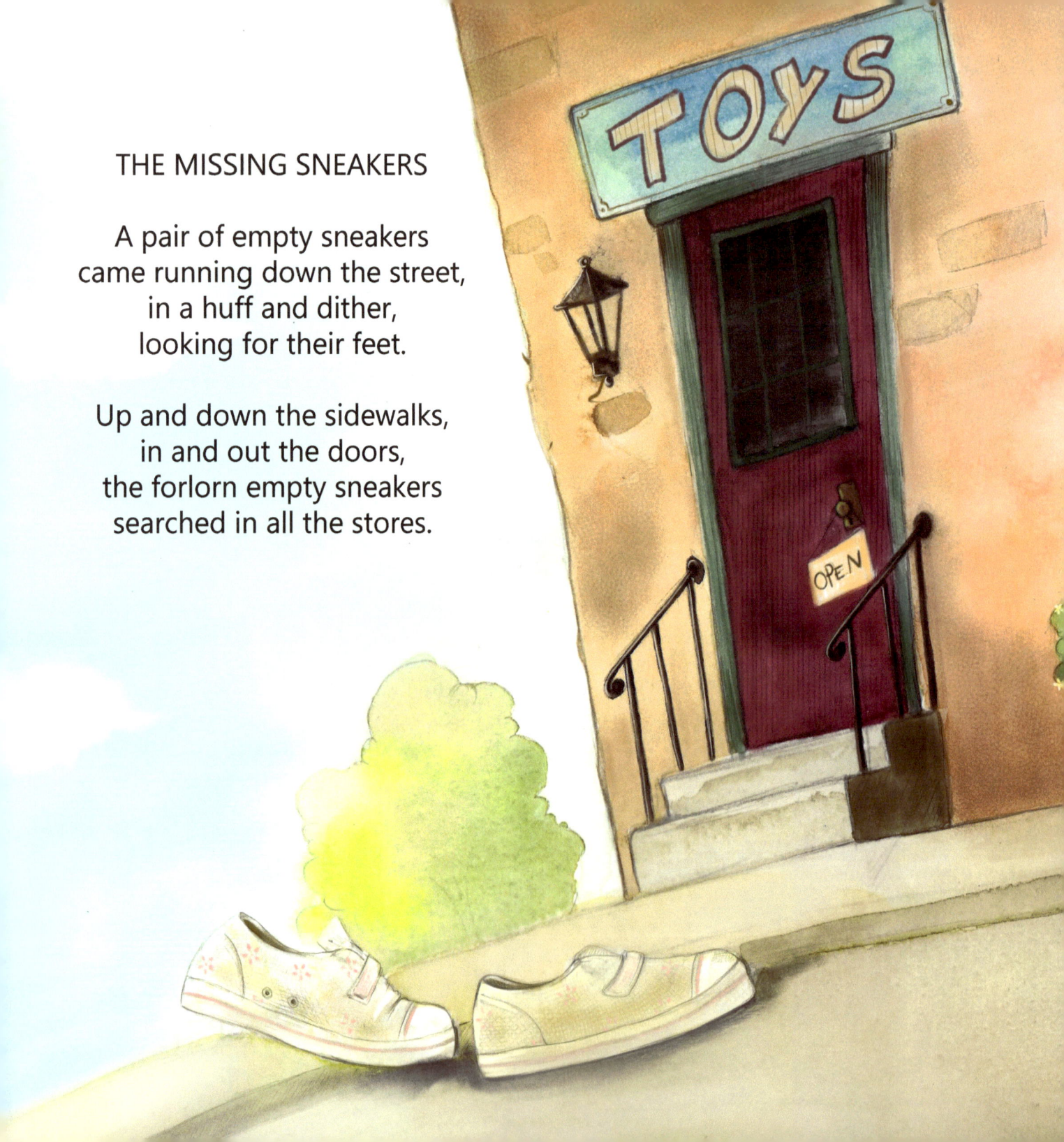

THE MISSING SNEAKERS

A pair of empty sneakers
came running down the street,
in a huff and dither,
looking for their feet.

Up and down the sidewalks,
in and out the doors,
the forlorn empty sneakers
searched in all the stores.

Then they reached the toy shop,
high upon the hill,
where they found Rebecca
sitting on a sill.

Laughing in the sunshine,
dangling her bare feet,
she espied the sneakers
standing in the street.

Oh!" she said. "My sneakers!
Now I am complete!"
Jumping down to greet them,
she slid them on her feet.

THE JUMP-JUMP GAME

Jump, jump,
Clap, clap,
Touch the sky,
Then touch your lap.

Jump, Jump,
Clap, clap,
Point your toe
And give a tap.

Jump, jump
Clap, clap,
Time to take
A cozy nap.

IF I WERE . . .

If I were a number,
I'd be a tall seven
that stands on the earth with
its head touching heaven.

If I were a letter,
I'd be a fine Y
that starts the word *yo-yo*
and ends the word *try*.

If I were a color,
I'd be a bright red,
as red as the apple
on Junior Tell's head.

But I'm not a number,
and I'm not a letter,
and I'm not a color,
No! I'm something better!

For I am a person
who laughs and who sings.
God gave me two feet and
two hands 'stead of wings.

I jump and I run,
and I laugh and have fun,
'cause God made me special
and clever!

BELIEVE AND SEE

Bumblebees,
in the sky,
do not know
they cannot fly.

If you tell them,
they will say,
they can do it
anyway.